fox keeping its cool

upset photographer

quick exit

help!

an unexpected visitor

surprise in store

helpful moose

Rand McNally's
Wonderful World
WORD BOOK
Illustrated by Hutchings

toucan

brown bear

grapes

elephant

rhinoceros

Rand McNally & Company
CHICAGO/NEW YORK/SAN FRANCISCO

empty gasoline
can

oranges

corn

apples

carrots

pears

Flowers

Inside a flower

petal

sepal

stamen

lazy gardner

In the fields . . .

cornflower

four-leaved clover

leaf

poppy

buttercup

daisy

By the stream . . .

forget-me-not

wood sorrel

lady's smock

waterlily

cowslip

In the woods . . .

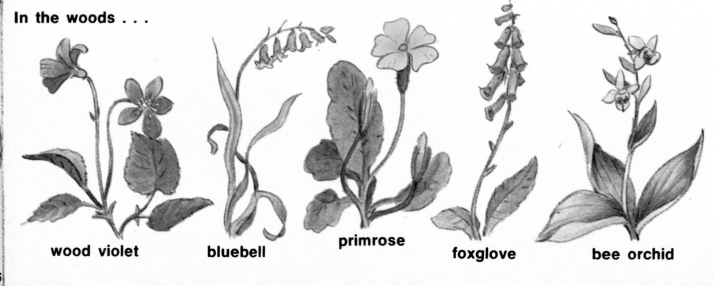

wood violet

bluebell

primrose

foxglove

bee orchid

6

Along the road . . .

bindweed stitchwort dandelion thistle ragwort

caterpillar

In the garden . . .

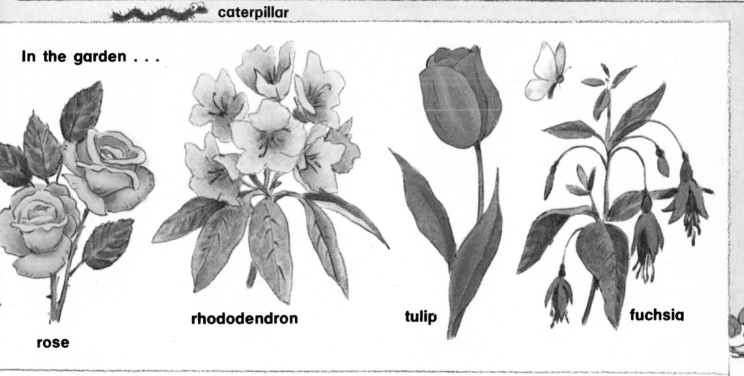

rose rhododendron tulip fuchsia

In the garden . . .

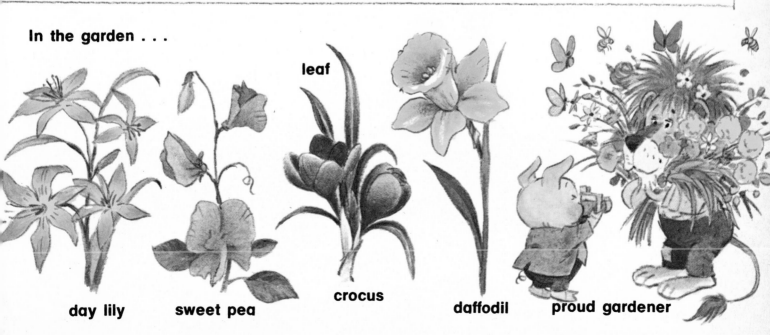

leaf

day lily sweet pea crocus daffodil proud gardener

7

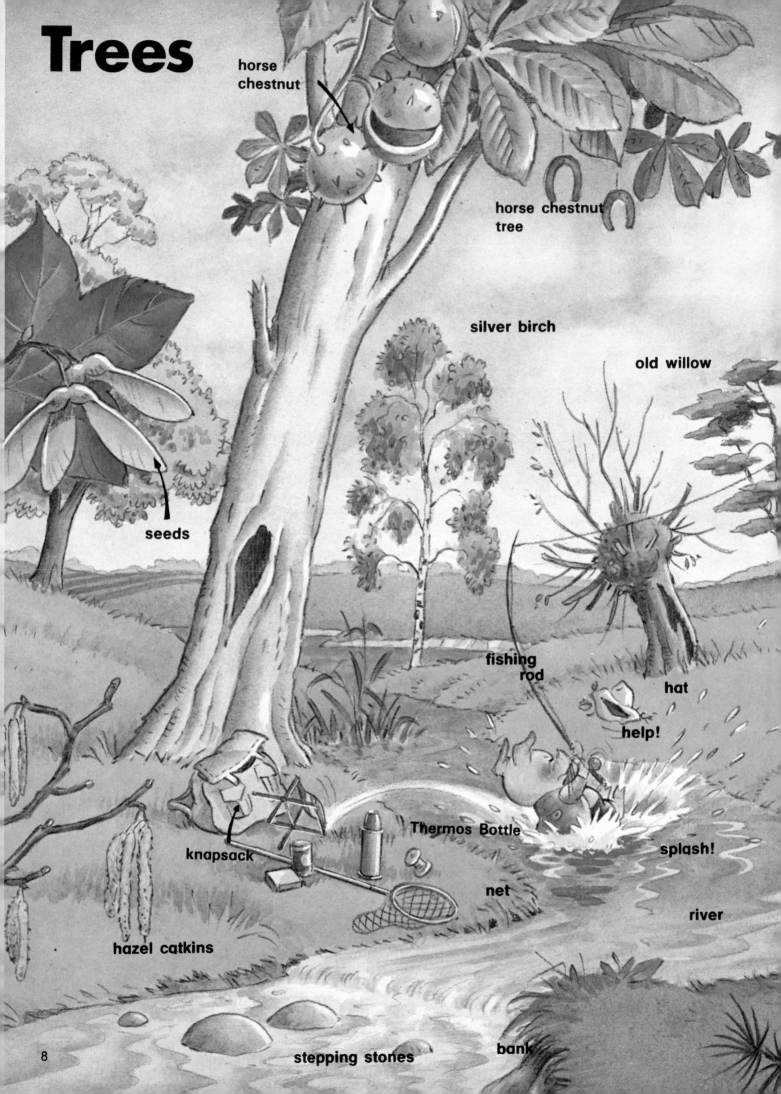

Trees

horse chestnut

horse chestnut tree

silver birch

old willow

seeds

fishing rod

hat

help!

knapsack

Thermos Bottle

splash!

net

river

hazel catkins

stepping stones

bank

8

leaves

heron

fish

fishing line

English elm

Scotch pine

spruce

cedar

oak

picnic basket

another hat

Jeep

holly bush

holly berries

reeds

larch pine

oak leaves

acorn

cone

9

Plants We Eat

apple

apple cut in half

blossom

bananas

banana tree

melons

strawberries

wheat

oats

pineapple

pineapple cut in half

cucumbers

beans

peas

tangerine

grapefruit

oranges

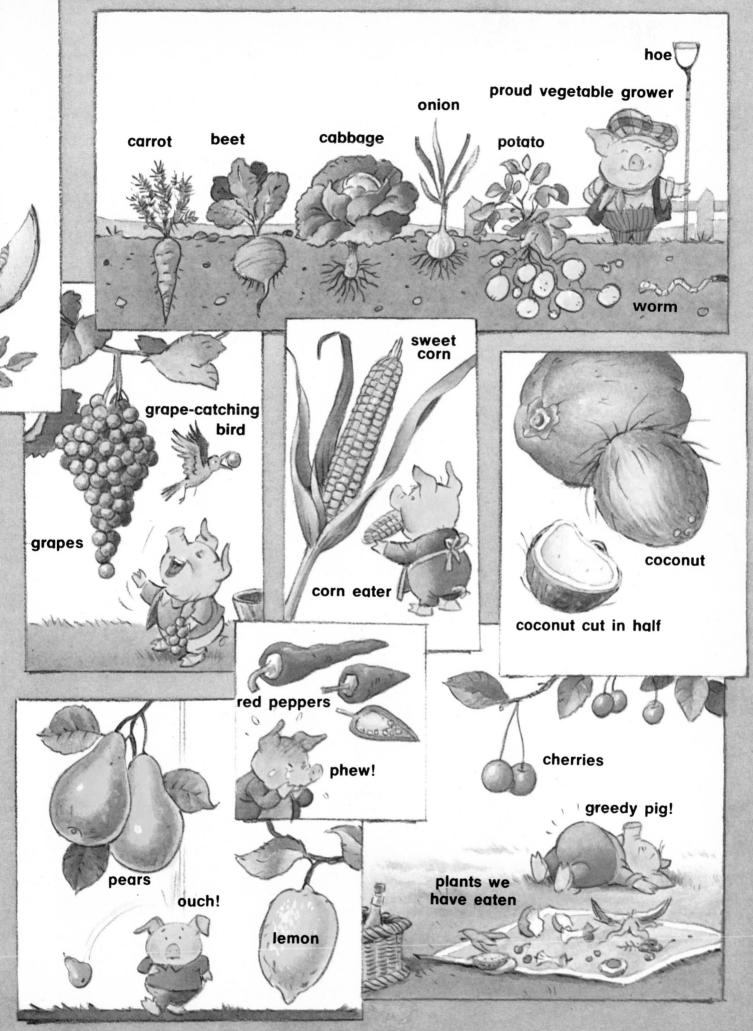

carrot

beet

cabbage

onion

potato

proud vegetable grower

hoe

worm

grapes

grape-catching bird

sweet corn

corn eater

coconut

coconut cut in half

red peppers

phew!

cherries

greedy pig!

pears

ouch!

lemon

plants we have eaten

11

Fungi and Cacti

shaggy ink cap

fly agaric

nature photographer

common mushrooms

camera

ladybugs

gypsy fungus

rain

umbrella

parasol mushroom

wood blewits

brownie cap

earth star

common morel

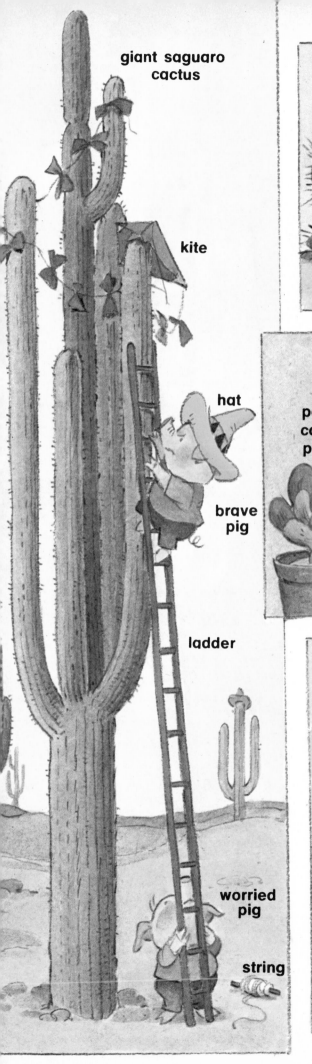

giant saguaro
cactus

kite

hat

brave
pig

ladder

worried
pig

string

prickly cactus

prickly porcupine

potted
cactus
plants

proud gardener

desert

tortoise waits for
turn in the shade

prickly pear
cactus

Tree Life

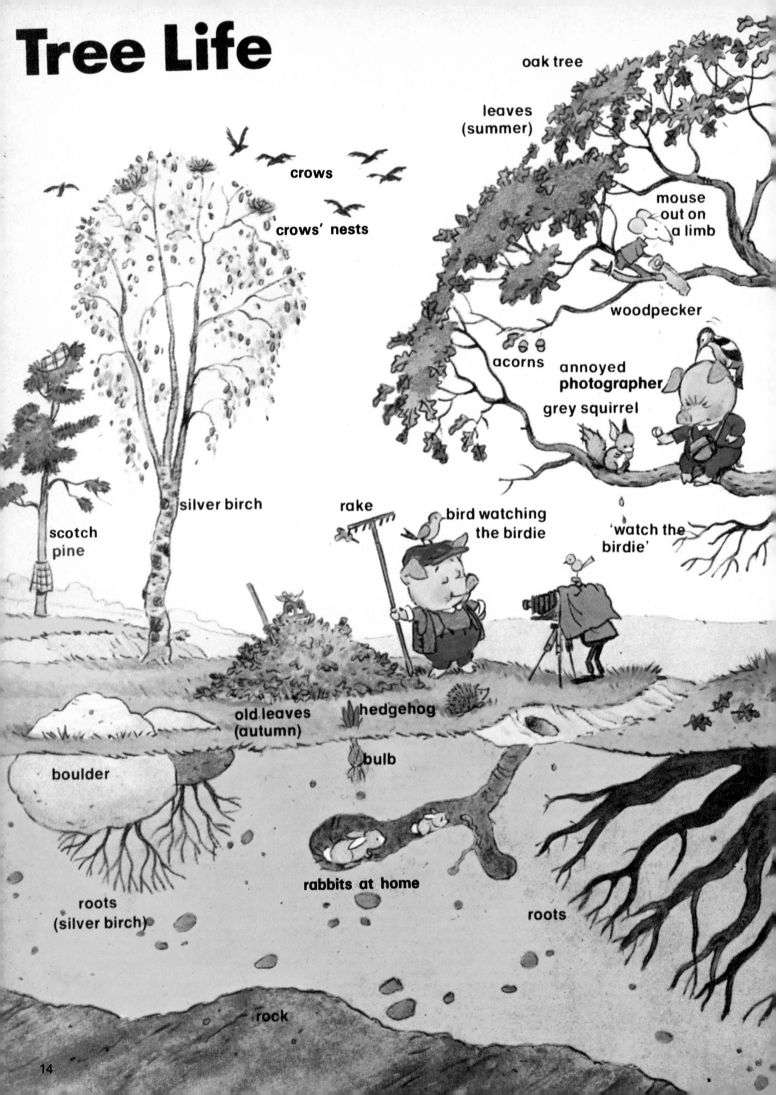

oak tree

leaves
(summer)

crows

crows' nests

mouse
out on
a limb

woodpecker

acorns

annoyed
photographer

grey squirrel

silver birch

rake

bird watching
the birdie

'watch the
birdie'

scotch
pine

old leaves
(autumn)

hedgehog

boulder

bulb

roots
(silver birch)

rabbits at home

roots

rock

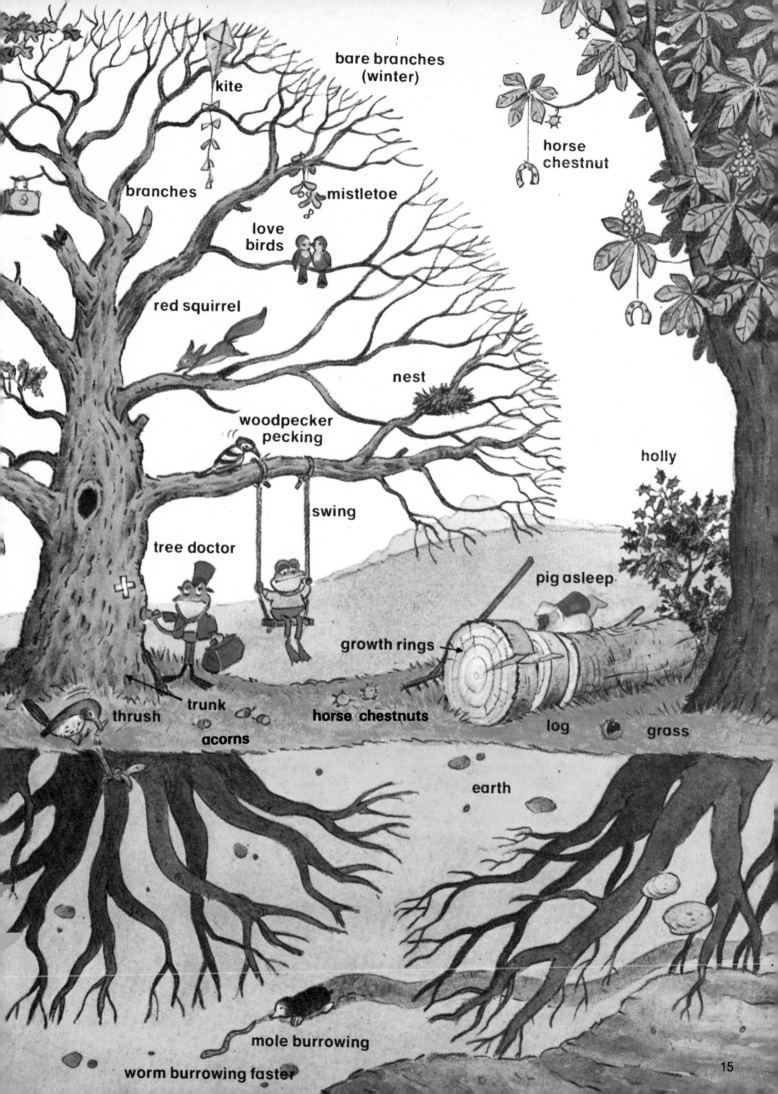

kite

bare branches
(winter)

horse
chestnut

branches

mistletoe

love
birds

red squirrel

nest

woodpecker
pecking

holly

swing

tree doctor

pig asleep

growth rings

thrush

trunk

horse chestnuts

log

grass

acorns

earth

mole burrowing

worm burrowing faster

15

Pets

German shepherd

crook

small chihuahua

bone

deerstalker hat

bloodhound

sheepdog

Persian cat

Scottie

Pekingese

collie

Siamese cat

kitten

basket

ear

tail

collar

nose

large mixed breed

muzzle

greyhound

thin body for running fast

bowler
hat

paw

leg

English bulldog

cocker
spaniel

poodle

basset hound

guinea pig

17

Wild Animals

blossom

baobab tree

leopard

cliff

another frightened
photographer

fast run

cheetah

tiger

movie camera

waterfall

rock

pride of lions

follow the
leader

safari Jeep

frightened
photographer

photo frog

rubber duck

spines

alligator

scared rat

porcupine

gibbon

hoopla!

giraffe

see the tongue?

smoke signals

neck

sliding gibbon

elephant

banana tree

ear

trunk

leaves

tail

cross pig

squashed camera

rhinoceros

exposed film

naughty mouse

warthog

19

sky

leaves

beech nut

pigeons

farmhouse

elm tree

trees

window

distant fields

field

Dutch barn

haystacks

angry bull

farmer

path

wall

gate

film

broken fence

movie camera

hat

pitchfork

sacks

step

fast-moving Jeep

puddle

cat

feather

chickens

21

Did You Know...?

the giraffe is the tallest animal—more than 19 feet tall

whoa!

boo!

an ostrich is the heaviest bird but it can't fly

swallowed camera

a bustard is the heaviest bird that flies

annoyed photographer

toothache

the wandering albatross has the longest wing span—about 11½ feet

the swift is the fastest flying bird—more than 95 m.p.h.

the blue whale is the largest animal—about 98 feet long

icebergs

it can weigh 140 tons

more than
350 feet
tall

kite

the redwood is
the tallest tree

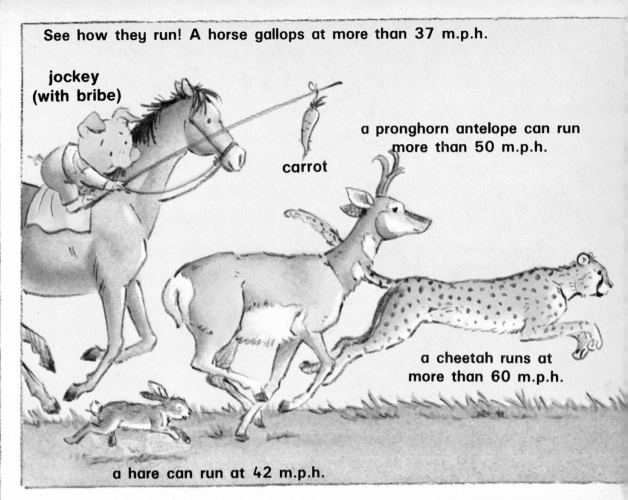

See how they run! A horse gallops at more than 37 m.p.h.

jockey
(with bribe)

carrot

a pronghorn antelope can run
more than 50 m.p.h.

a cheetah runs at
more than 60 m.p.h.

a hare can run at 42 m.p.h.

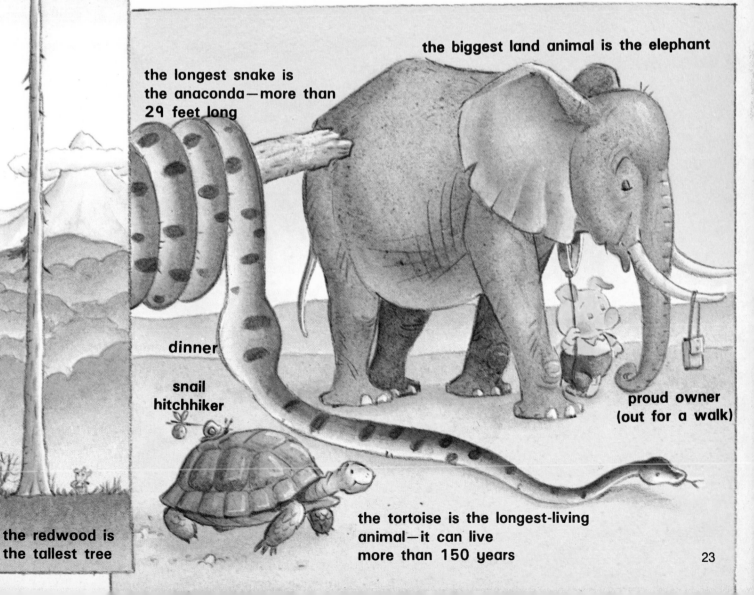

the biggest land animal is the elephant

the longest snake is
the anaconda—more than
29 feet long

dinner

snail
hitchhiker

proud owner
(out for a walk)

the tortoise is the longest-living
animal—it can live
more than 150 years

Creatures at Home

eagles' eyrie

nesting swifts

squirrel

bird on nest

bear leaving den

rabbit burrow

snail in shell

bank

twigs

beavers in
a lodge

underwater

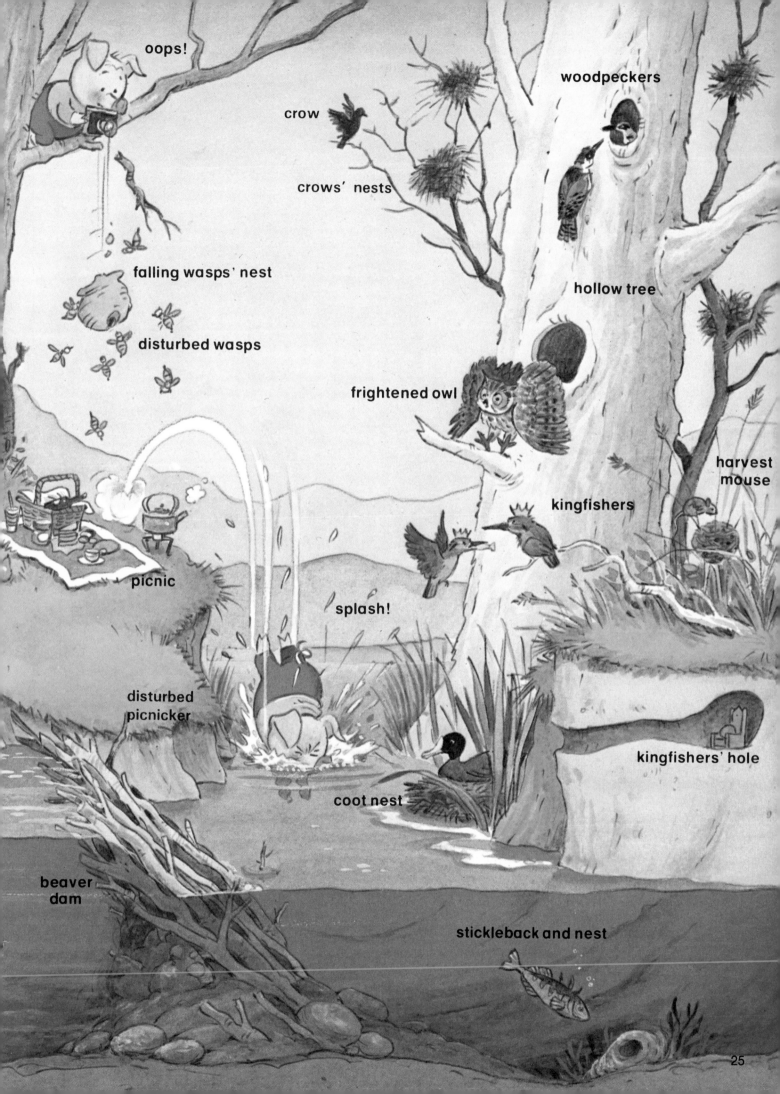

Birds

little owl

bird kite

swift swift

long-eared owl

sparrow hawk

cuckoo

kingfisher

two toucans

frightened frog

balloon-pecking bird

ladybug

balloon

fishing rod

ride 'em frog

flamingo

cassowary

shoe

flightless kiwi

hat

boot

fisherman with catch

photographer pig

watch the birdie!

storks

golden eagle

ostrich

exposed film

macaw

branch

pecking
woodpecker

swallowed
camera

emperor penguin
(on vacation from
the Antarctic)

mom duck

duckling

ostrich
chick

fairy penguin

ostrich eggs

27

Feet, Wings and Beaks

slim wing

wandering albatross

broad wing

South American condor

pheasant

cuckoo

swallow

hang glider

bird of paradise

tail

upside-down bird of paradise

tuning fork

humming bird

pig photographer in hiding

pelican

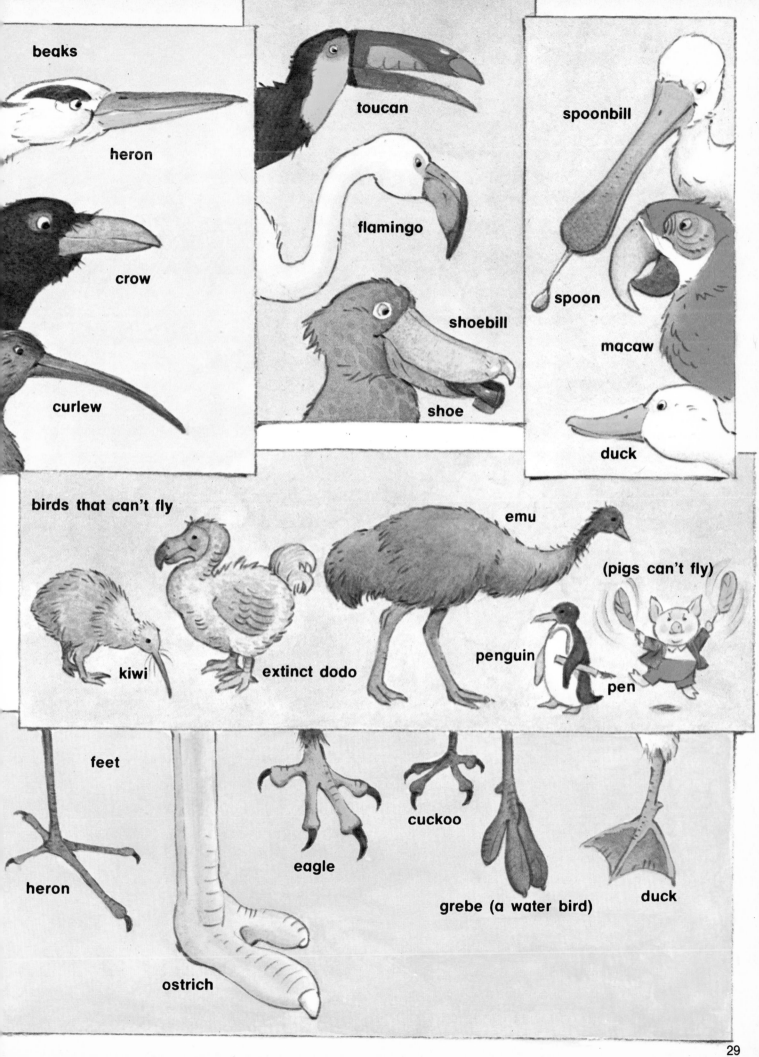

beaks

heron

toucan

spoonbill

flamingo

crow

shoebill

spoon

macaw

shoe

curlew

duck

birds that can't fly

emu

(pigs can't fly)

kiwi

extinct dodo

penguin

pen

feet

heron

eagle

cuckoo

grebe (a water bird)

duck

ostrich

29

Insects

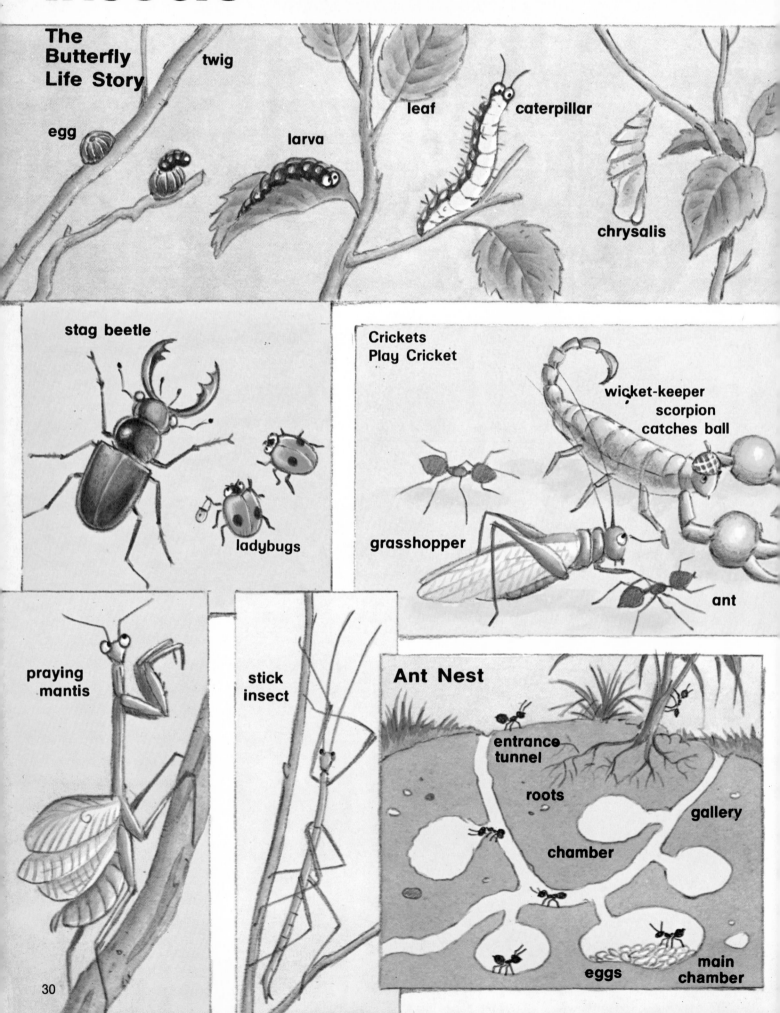

The Butterfly Life Story

twig

egg

larva

leaf

caterpillar

chrysalis

stag beetle

ladybugs

Crickets Play Cricket

wicket-keeper scorpion catches ball

grasshopper

ant

praying mantis

stick insect

Ant Nest

entrance tunnel

roots

chamber

gallery

eggs

main chamber

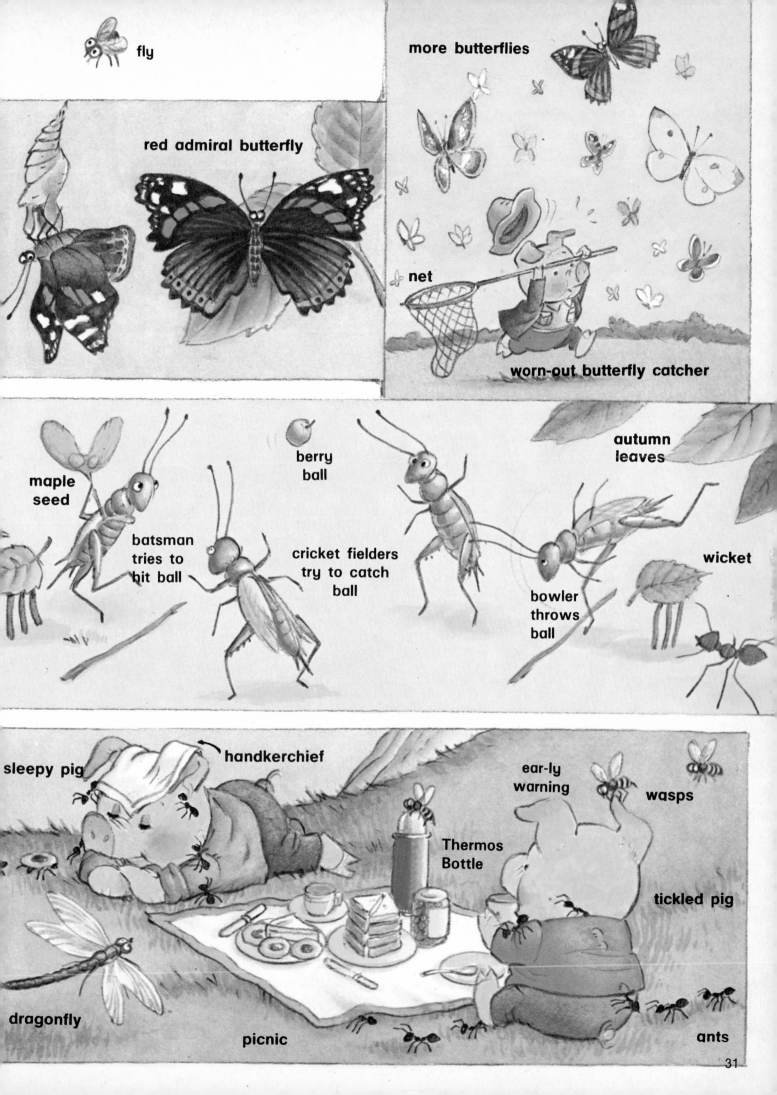

fly

more butterflies

red admiral butterfly

net

worn-out butterfly catcher

maple seed

berry ball

autumn leaves

batsman tries to hit ball

cricket fielders try to catch ball

bowler throws ball

wicket

handkerchief

sleepy pig

ear-ly warning

wasps

Thermos Bottle

tickled pig

dragonfly

picnic

ants

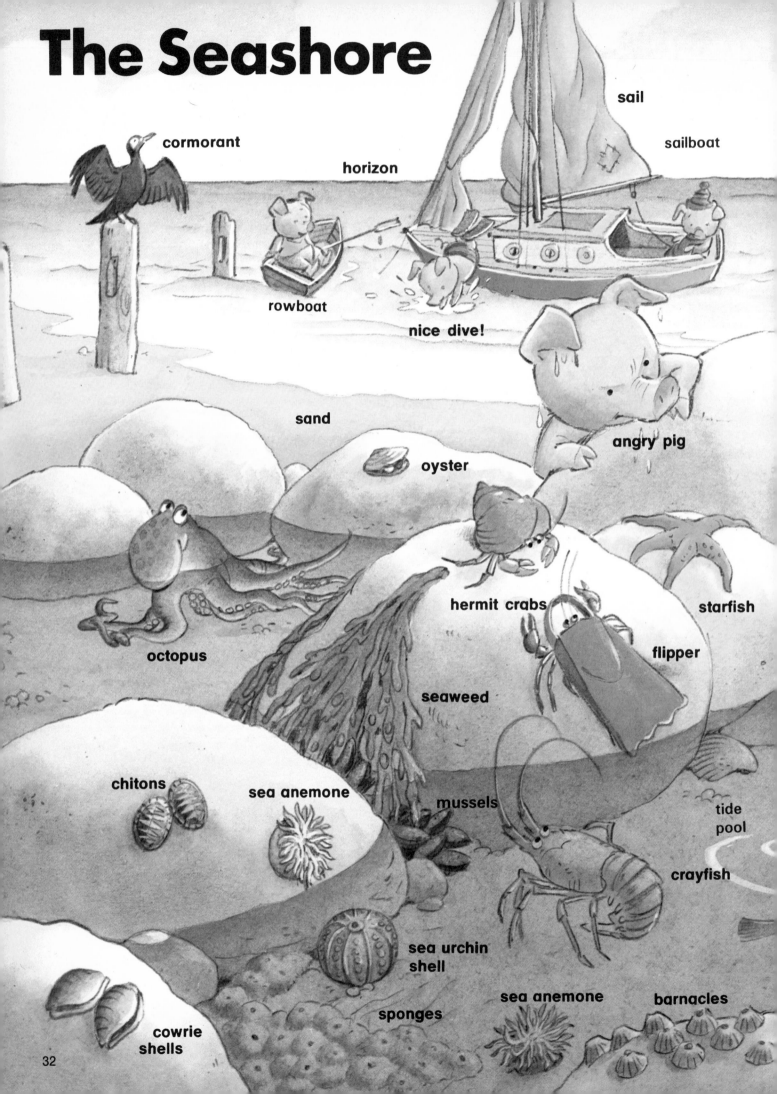

The Seashore

sail

sailboat

cormorant

horizon

rowboat

nice dive!

sand

oyster

angry pig

hermit crabs

starfish

octopus

flipper

seaweed

chitons

sea anemone

mussels

tide pool

crayfish

sea urchin shell

sea anemone

barnacles

sponges

cowrie shells

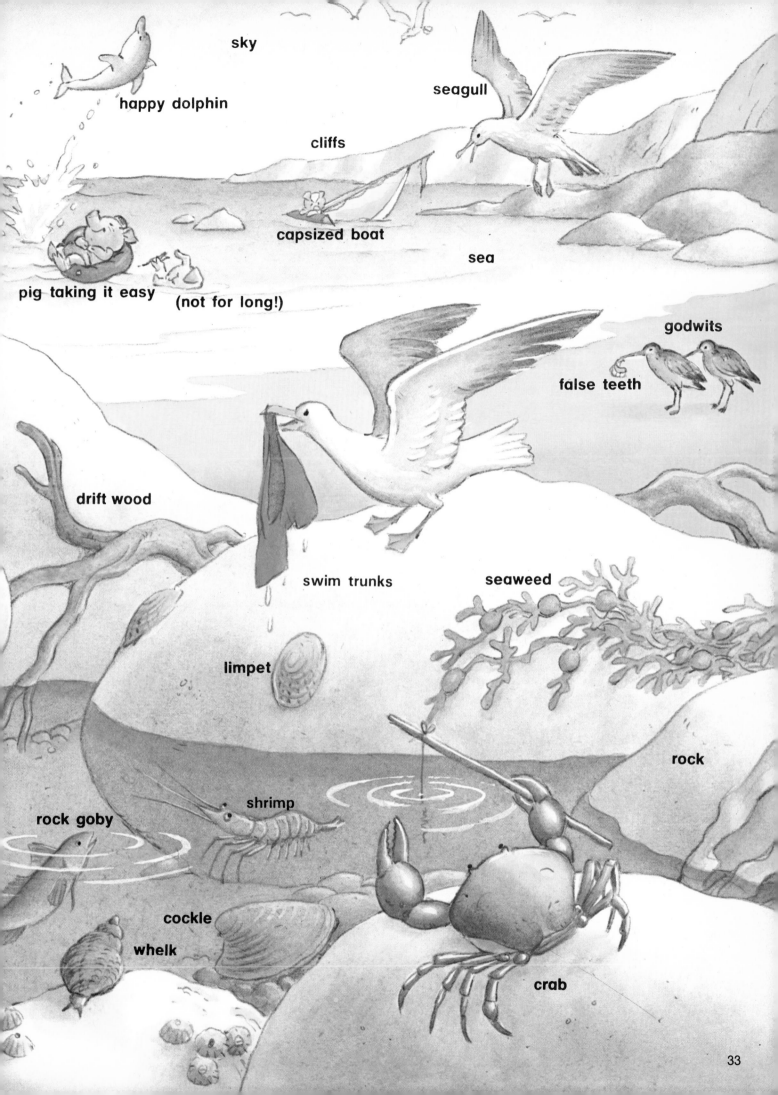

sky

happy dolphin

seagull

cliffs

capsized boat

sea

pig taking it easy

(not for long!)

godwits

false teeth

drift wood

swim trunks

seaweed

limpet

rock

rock goby

shrimp

cockle

whelk

crab

33

In the Mountains

eagle

moving movie photographer

bear cub

bears

moose

distant hills

photographer in disguise

rabbit

little owl having a ride

owl.

ibex

chicks

another photographer in disguise

eagle's eyrie

hat

mountain goat

bats in a cave

bush

red squirrel

pine cone

boulder

35

saguaro cactus

condor

burro

sand

coyote

rattlesnake

yucca plant

cactus

camel

camera

desert tortoise

elf owls

road runner

kangaroo rat

another lizard

37

Pond

mallard duck

bull rushes

swallow

swinging mouse in for a wet time

pig reading

follow the reader

buttercups

ant

caterpillar

moorhen

swan swimming

water lilies

reeds

eggs

duck ducking

frog

tadpoles

pond snail

old boot

wheel

water scorpion

kingfisher

willow tree

willow
leaves

photographer
in a hideout

snap!

bank

dragonfly

yellow wagtail

pigs up a pole

sand martin

punting

tin
can

heron fishing

water
crowfoot

rushes

eel grass

water beetle

stickleback

newt

water vole

roots

39

Under the Sea

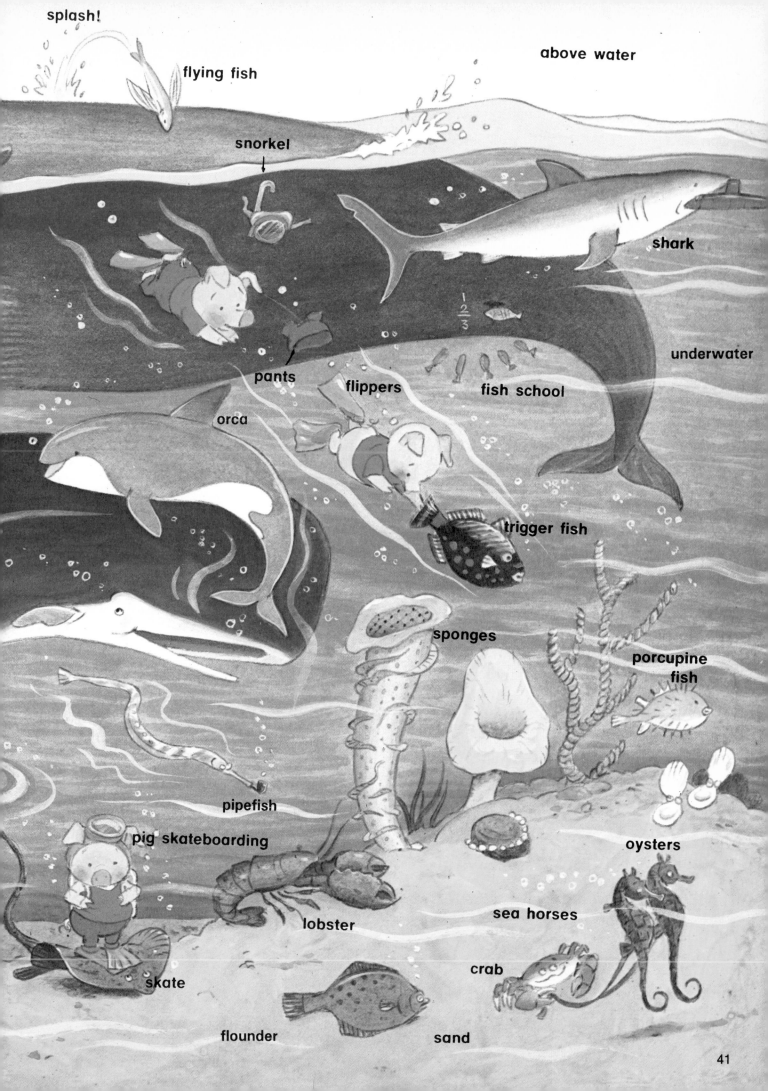

splash!

flying fish

above water

snorkel

shark

underwater

pants

flippers

fish school

orca

trigger fish

sponges

porcupine
fish

pipefish

pig skateboarding

oysters

sea horses

lobster

skate

crab

flounder

sand

surefooted dog sled

get back!

ice pack

igloo

polar bear

seal nosedive

splash!

cold sea

squid

penguin photographer

dressed up like an Eskimo

baby penguin on sled

43

Jungle

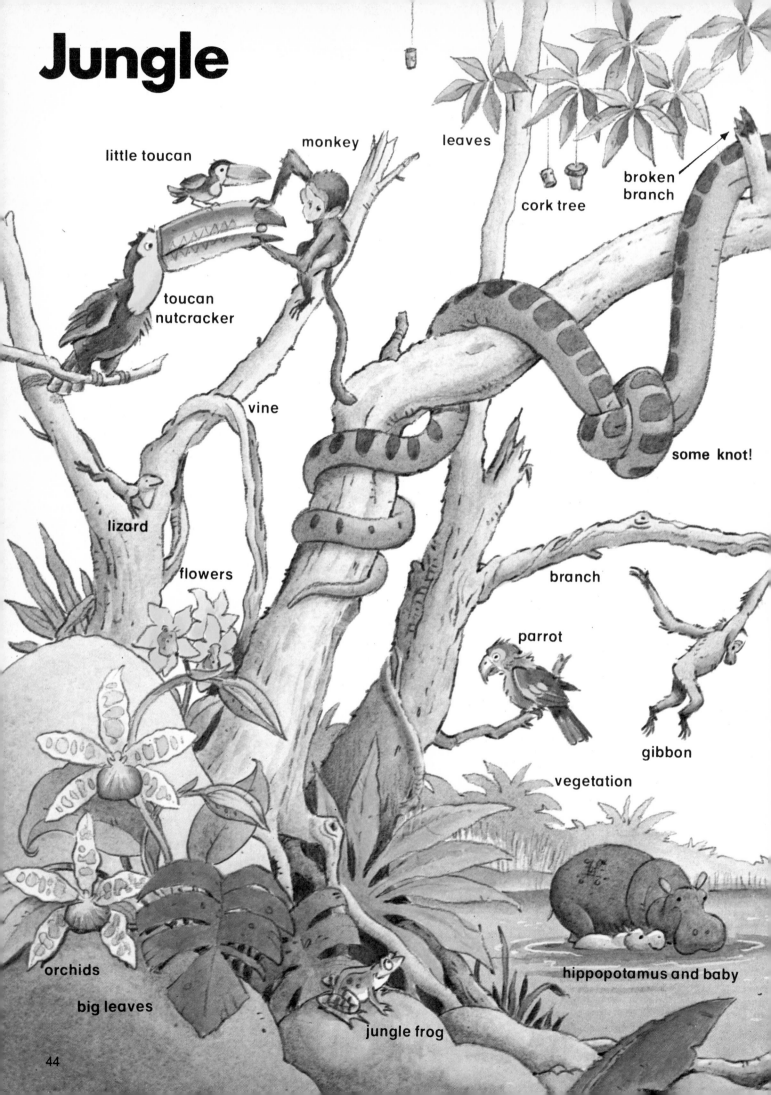

little toucan

monkey

leaves

broken branch

cork tree

toucan nutcracker

vine

some knot!

lizard

flowers

branch

parrot

gibbon

vegetation

orchids

big leaves

jungle frog

hippopotamus and baby

python

forked
tongue

vines

**fern
leaves**

big tree

hornbill

chimpanzee
eating a
banana

a naughty gibbon

camera

swinging pig

palm trees

**roots of
fallen tree**

smoke

tiger

funnel

wobbly
photographer

river boat

butterfly

rock

swamp

scorpion

crocodile

root

fern leaves

Camouflage

moth

spotted deer

oh dear!

striped tiger

where is it?

bittern

frog

photographers camouflaged as trees

woodpecker

chameleon

nightjar

smile please!

what's this?

crocodile

polar bears

moving house

47

Weather

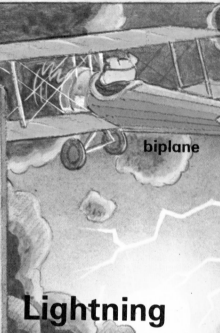

biplane

Lightning

Sunset

Snow

mouse

snowball

snow

Mist

mist

Rain

umbrella

puddles

Storm at Sea

smoke

gull

boat

wave

sea

caterpillar

Hurricane

palm trees

straw huts

ilhouette

Clouds

cumulus

stratus clouds

drip

Tornado

dust clouds

help!

Photographic Exhibition
1
2
3
4

onlooker puddles

tail

Volcanoes

seagull coughing

park ranger

posting danger sign

vulture

mallet

photographers' club

whomp!

crack!

butterfly

falling photographers?

frightened tarantula

pancake-catching bird

landslide

falling rocks

worried frog

chef's hat

another pancake

heavy sleeper

cook

oops!

bowl of pancake batter

pancake

mouse

table

baby volcano

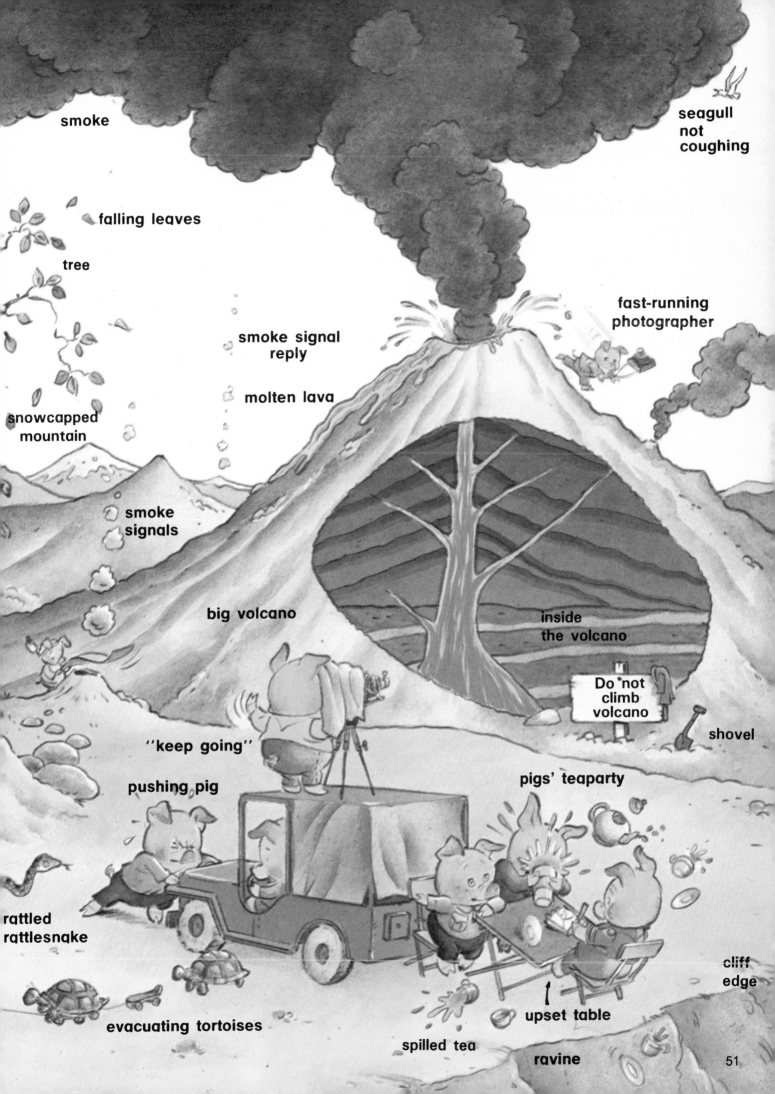

River

rain

mountains

glacier

cold lake

waterfall

rock face

hilltop

grizzly bear

ravine

hill

rock

tributary

moose

fox

boulders

clouds

golden eagle

mounted camera

mountain

wing

worried pilot

tail

wing

biplane

look!

froggy filming

stream

river mouth

delta

estuary

shore

islands

sea

53

Asia

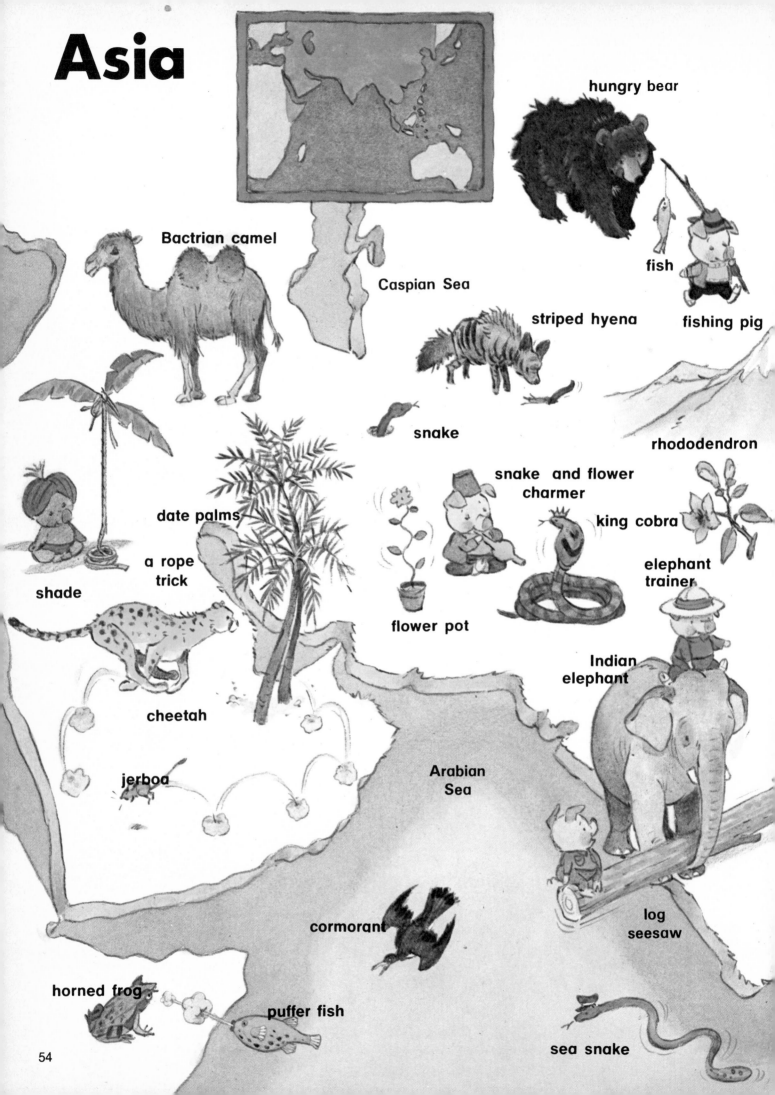

hungry bear

Bactrian camel

Caspian Sea

fish

fishing pig

striped hyena

snake

rhododendron

snake and flower charmer

date palms

king cobra

a rope trick

flower pot

elephant trainer

shade

cheetah

Indian elephant

jerboa

Arabian Sea

cormorant

log seesaw

horned frog

puffer fish

sea snake

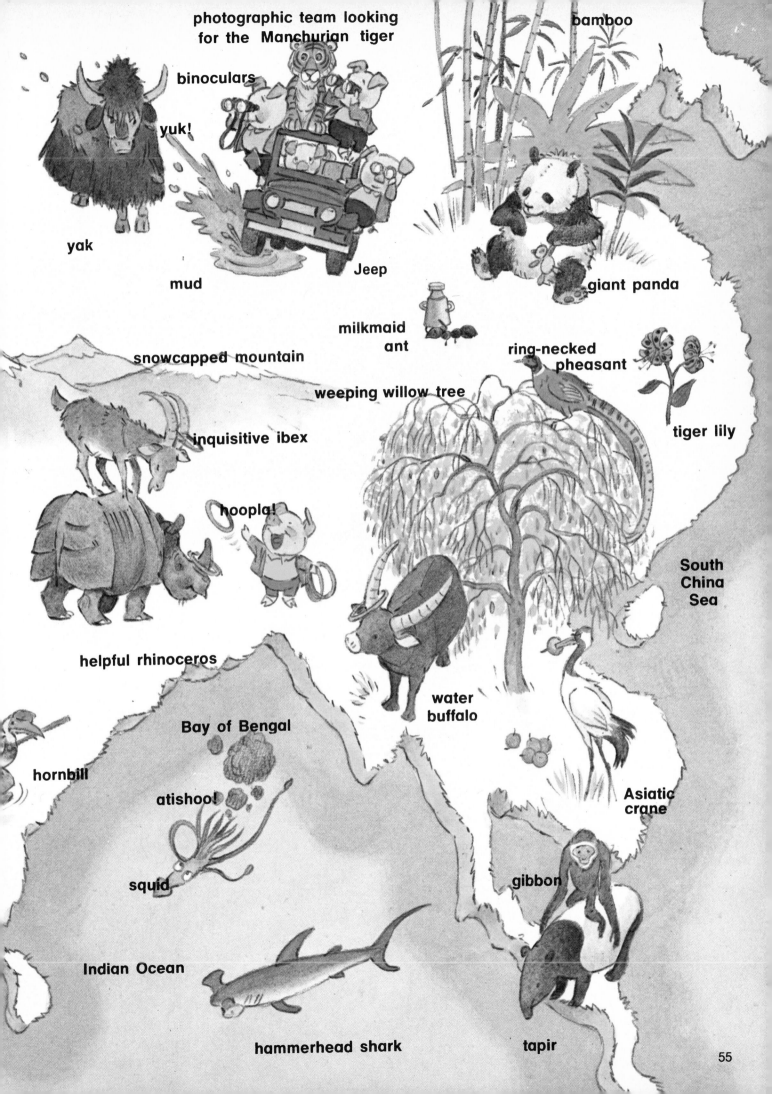

photographic team looking for the Manchurian tiger

bamboo

binoculars

yuk!

yak

mud

Jeep

giant panda

milkmaid ant

ring-necked pheasant

snowcapped mountain

weeping willow tree

tiger lily

inquisitive ibex

hoopla!

South China Sea

helpful rhinoceros

water buffalo

Bay of Bengal

hornbill

atishoo!

Asiatic crane

squid

gibbon

Indian Ocean

hammerhead shark

tapir

55

Africa

elephant

hat

dates

upset photographer

squashed camera

sand dunes

camel

large python

small oasis

date palm

rhinoceros

warthog

palm leaves

photographers in disguise

smile!

crocodile

sailboat

Atlantic Ocean

octopus

what's that?

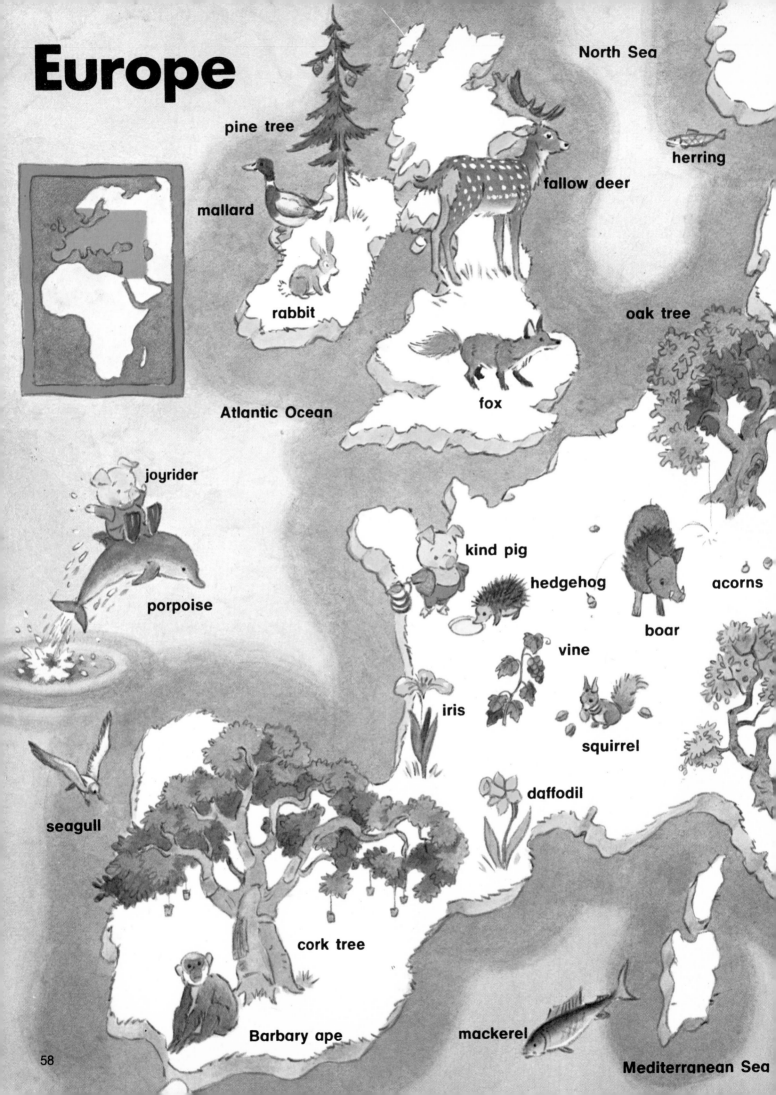

Europe

pine tree

North Sea

mallard

fallow deer

herring

rabbit

oak tree

fox

Atlantic Ocean

joyrider

kind pig

hedgehog

acorns

porpoise

boar

vine

iris

squirrel

daffodil

seagull

cork tree

Barbary ape

mackerel

Mediterranean Sea

Australia

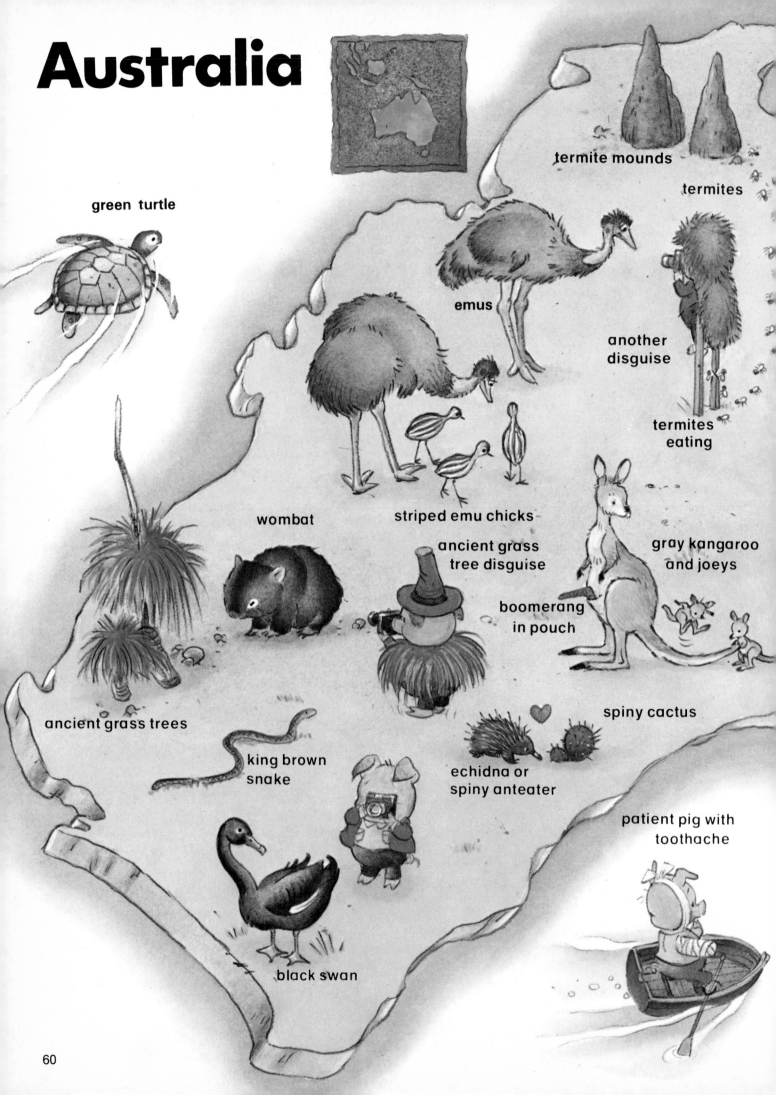

green turtle

termite mounds

termites

emus

another disguise

termites eating

wombat

striped emu chicks

ancient grass tree disguise

gray kangaroo and joeys

boomerang in pouch

ancient grass trees

spiny cactus

king brown snake

echidna or spiny anteater

patient pig with toothache

black swan

cockatiels

red desert kangaroos

branch breaking

kookaburra laughing (but not for long)

pogo stick

koala

gum trees or eucalyptus trees

bark

hat with corks

rocks

springy feet

platypus

Pacific Ocean

gray nurse shark

Tasmanian devil

checkered swallowtail

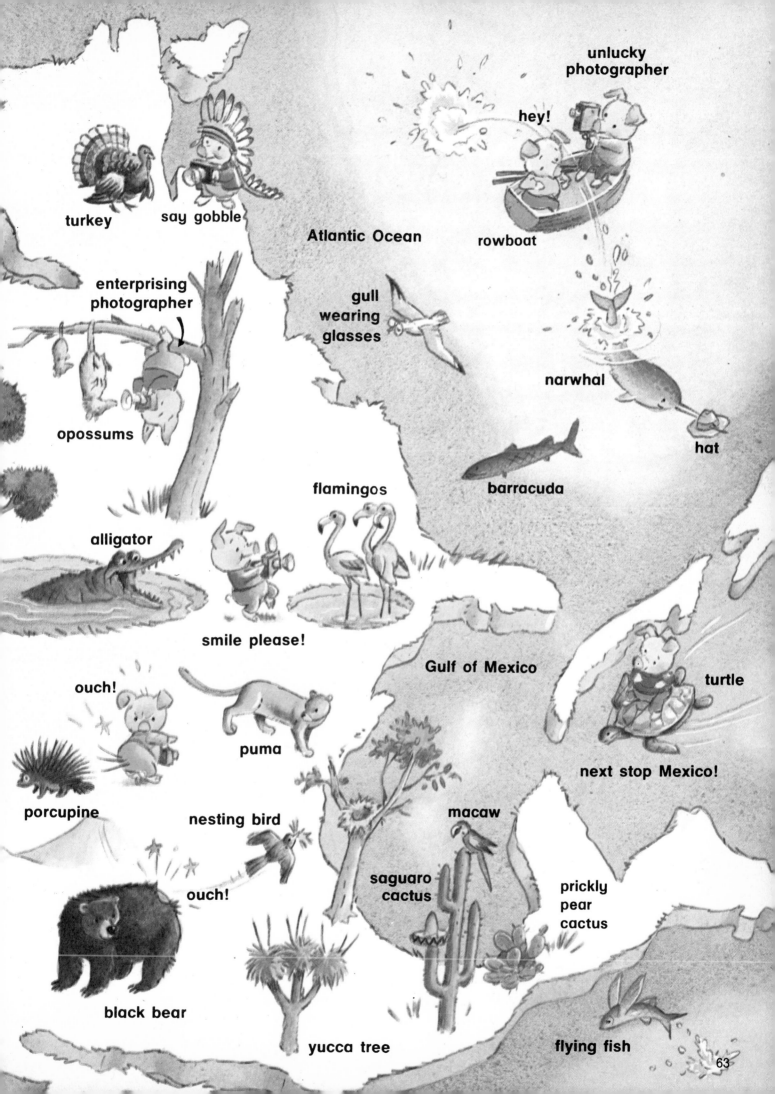

turkey

say gobble

unlucky photographer

hey!

Atlantic Ocean

rowboat

enterprising photographer

gull wearing glasses

narwhal

hat

opossums

barracuda

flamingos

alligator

smile please!

Gulf of Mexico

turtle

ouch!

puma

next stop Mexico!

porcupine

nesting bird

macaw

saguaro cactus

prickly pear cactus

ouch!

black bear

yucca tree

flying fish

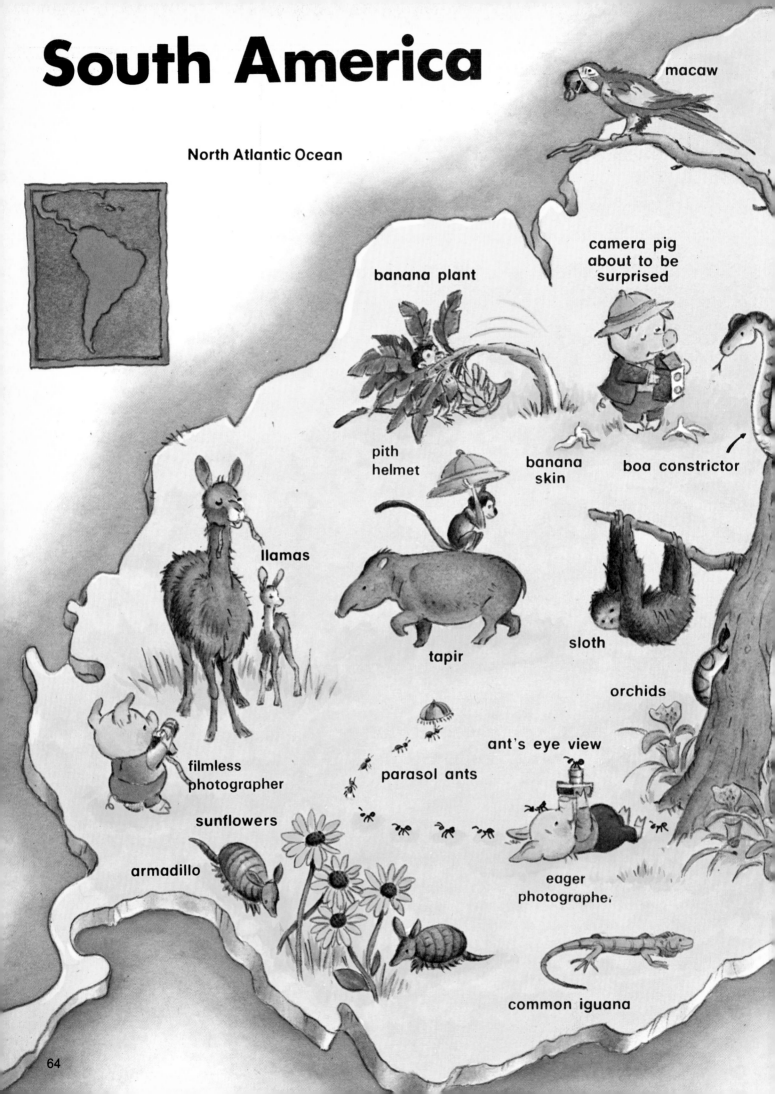

South America

North Atlantic Ocean

macaw

banana plant

camera pig about to be surprised

pith helmet

banana skin

boa constrictor

llamas

tapir

sloth

orchids

filmless photographer

ant's eye view

parasol ants

sunflowers

armadillo

eager photographer

common iguana

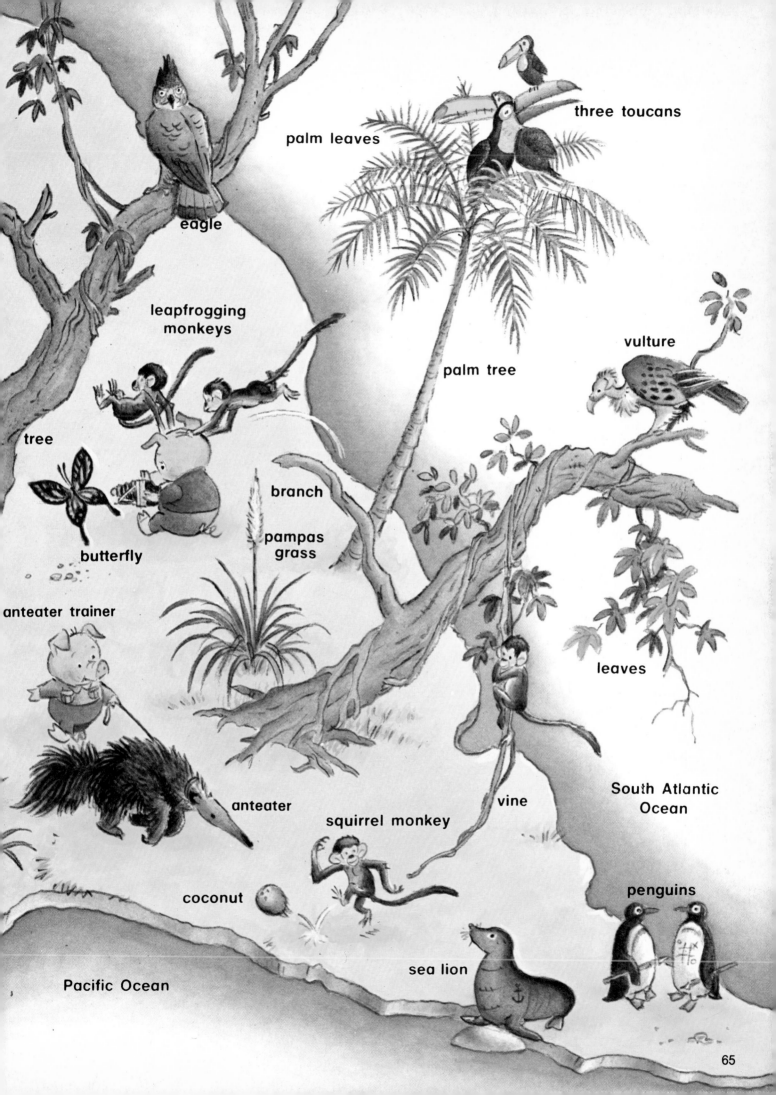

eagle

three toucans

palm leaves

leapfrogging
monkeys

vulture

palm tree

tree

branch

butterfly

pampas
grass

leaves

anteater trainer

South Atlantic
Ocean

anteater

vine

squirrel monkey

coconut

penguins

sea lion

Pacific Ocean

65

Day and Night

ducks

pink sky

sunrise

hills

reeds

water

antlers

mist

moose

movie camera on tripod

hat

yawn

dew drops on spider's web

decoy

pole

sleepy pigs

punt

Morning

palm tree

annoying mosquito

basket

shadows

kettle

pig sitting in shade

picnic

Evening

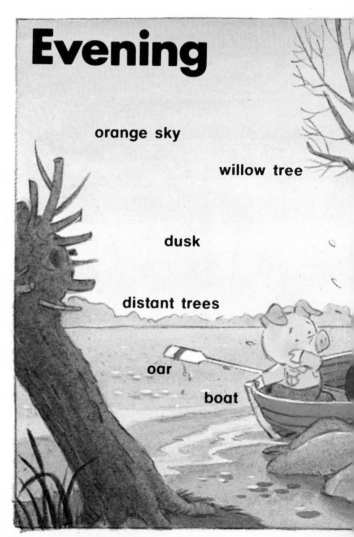

orange sky

willow tree

dusk

distant trees

oar

boat

blue sky

distant mountains

desert

cactus

camel

sand

Midday

branches

plate camera

wet poodle

grass

bank

boulder

Night

dark blue sky

bat

stars

branch

moon

owl

tree

fir trees

moonlight
reflection

nervous
pig

shadow

another nervous
pig

old log (or is it?)

Spring

fawn

picnic

cuckoo

rabbit

mouse

mole

birds

hazel catkins

fallen tree

rocks

above-water photographer

duck in nest

tin can

heron

violets

buttercups

reeds

snorkel

ears

underwater photographer

buds

pool

brown trout

twigs

68

leaves

mother duck
with ducklings

willow leaves

rock pool

birds' nest
with eggs

otter family

waterfall

magpie

coltsfoot

more
primroses

stones

primroses

69

leaves

clouds

silver birch tree

willow

sausages

heron

branch

Jeep

hedgehog

campion

flat tire

river

duck

water lilies

foxgloves

kingfisher

lapwing

polecat

roots

ladybugs

bindweed

boulders

piantain

71

sky

autumn leaves

ducks in formation

gray squirrel

silver birch

turtle dove

maple leaves

kingfisher

fungi

deer

stag

blackberries

pheasant

old willow stump

fungi

bracken

duck
swimming

fly
mushrooms

stream

73

Winter

snow falling

branches

weeping willow

cedar

wild duck

sedge grass

oak tree

snowballs

lake

cow parsley

blackbird

bird tracks

snow

otter

crocus

holly

snowdrops

74

crow

bare twigs

mistletoe

squirrel asleep

owl

sleigh

ice

buck

fox

fallow deer

robin

crows

old ferns

rabbit

75

Natural Curiosities

the father seahorse carries the babies in his pouch

these animals can carry their young on their backs

anteater

koala

hippopotamus

the kangaroo's baby is about 1½ inches long when born and is carried in mom's pouch

woodcock

some birds can carry their chicks while flying

odd pigeons

fantail

pouter

this angler fish has its own fishing line

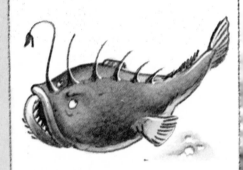

giant earthworms up to 11 feet long can be found in Australia

giraffes cannot reach the ground to drink unless they spread their front legs

their purple tongues are over 12 inches long

the camel can go without food for a long time—it stores fat in its humps

Bactrian camel

hollow bottle trees (baobab trees) can hold over 12 people—they have been used as prisons

the platypus has a leathery ducklike beak and webbed feet

New Zealand's tuatara lizard is a leftover from the age of dinosaurs

chameleons can change color to blend in with the background

a rhinoceros horn is made of the same things as hair and fingernails

the elephant has the longest nose and biggest ears of any animal

the smallest bird is a humming bird—it is not much bigger than the bee below

a carpenter bee